te Elementary to
rly Intermediate

HILARIOUS

MW00826430

AN COATES **POPULAR PIANO LIBRARY**

BOO

CONTENTS

The Aba-Daba Honeymoon 2

Barney Google 4

Be My Little Baby Bumblebee 6

Cheeseburger in Paradise 9

Does Your Chewing Gum Lose Its Flavor
on the Bedpost Overnight? 12

Doodle Doo Doo 14

Hello Muddah, Hello Fadduh! 16

Itsy Bitsy Teenie Weenie Yellow Polka Dot Bikini . . 20

Jeepers Creepers 24

Little Sir Echo 26

When Banana Skins Are Falling
(I'll Come Sliding Back to You) 29

ISBN-10: 0-7390-5334-5
ISBN-13: 978-0-7390-5334-8

Alfred

THE ABA-DABA HONEYMOON

Words and Music by
Arthur Fields and Walter Donovan
Arranged by Dan Coates

BARNEY GOOGLE

Words and Music by
Billy Rose and Con Conrad
Arranged by Dan Coates

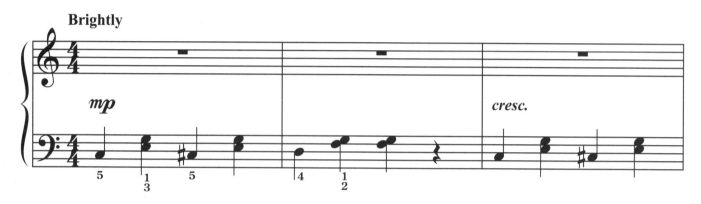

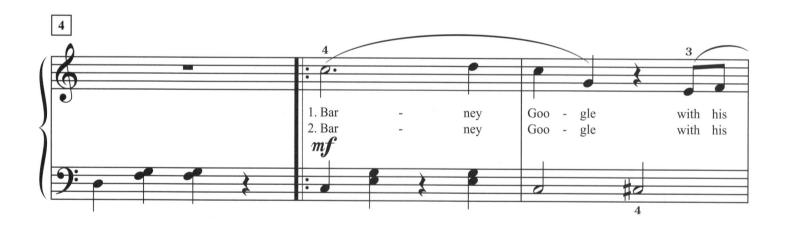

1. Bar - ney Goo - gle with his
2. Bar - ney Goo - gle with his

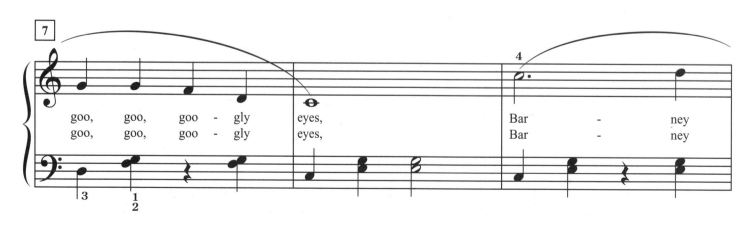

goo, goo, goo - gly eyes, Bar - ney
goo, goo, goo - gly eyes, Bar - ney

10

Goo - gle had a wife three times his size.
Goo - gle bet his horse would win the prize.

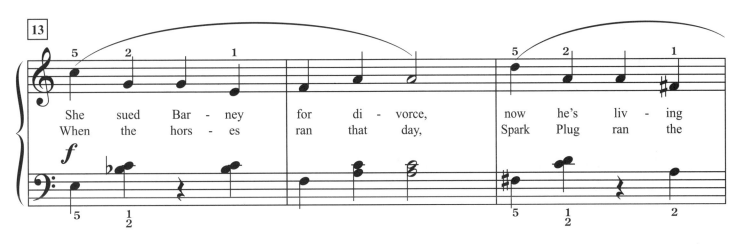

13

She sued Bar - ney for di - vorce, now he's liv - ing
When the hors - es ran that day, Spark Plug ran the

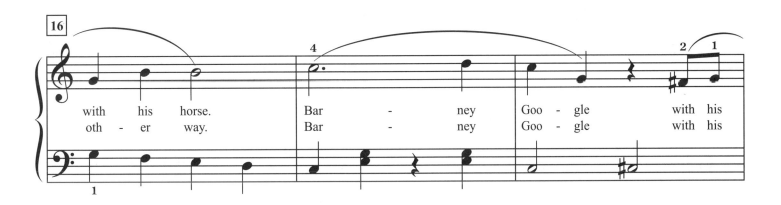

16

with his horse. Bar - ney Goo - gle with his
oth - er way. Bar - ney Goo - gle with his

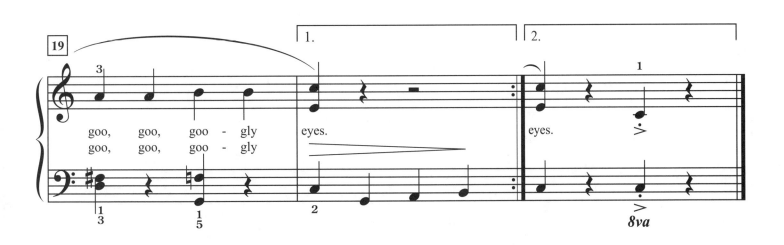

19

1.
2.

goo, goo, goo - gly eyes.
goo, goo, goo - gly eyes.

8va

BE MY LITTLE BABY BUMBLEBEE

Words and Music by
Stanley Murphy and Henry I. Marshall
Arranged by Dan Coates

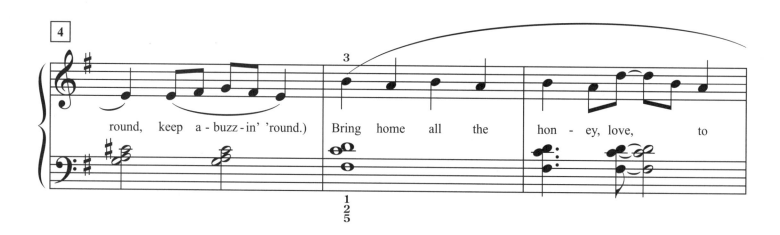

7

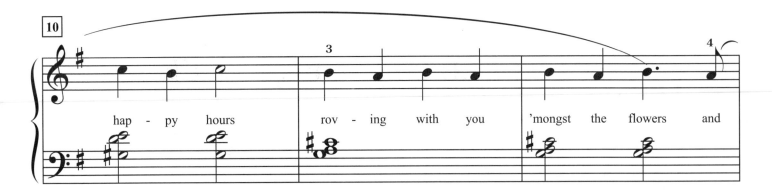

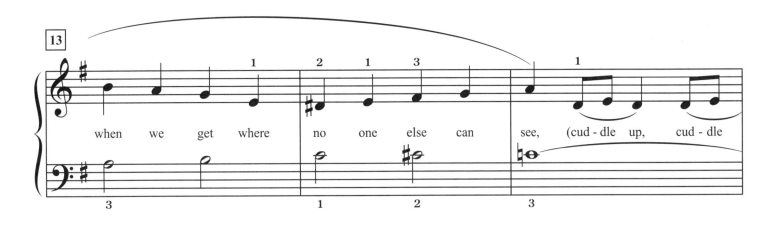

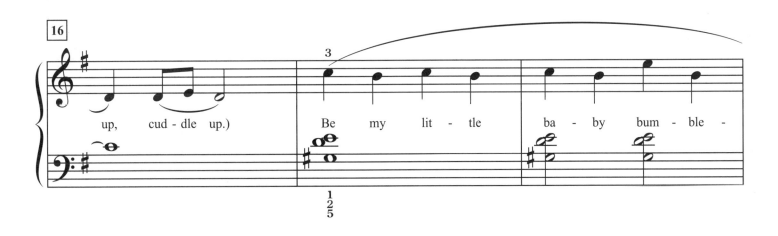

hap - py   as   can   be,   (you and me,   you and   me,   you and me.)

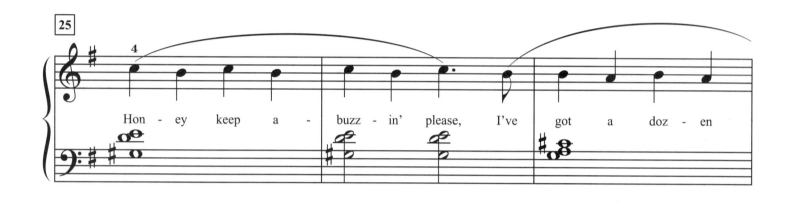

Hon - ey   keep   a -   buzz - in'   please,   I've   got   a   doz - en

cou - sin   bees,   but I   want   you   to   be   my   ba - by bum - ble -

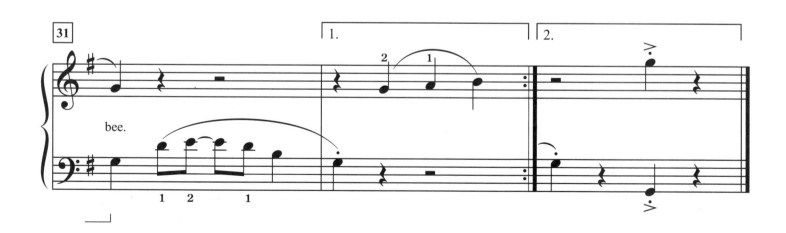

bee.

CHEESEBURGER IN PARADISE

Words and Music by Jimmy Buffett
Arranged by Dan Coates

Moderately, with a steady beat

Tried to a - mend my car - niv - o - rous hab - its.

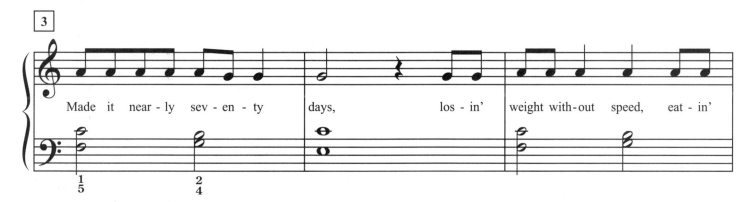

Made it near - ly sev - en - ty days, los - in' weight with - out speed, eat - in'

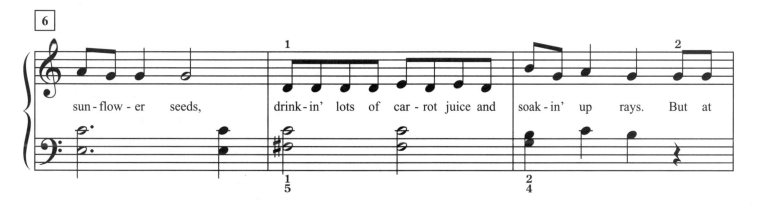

sun - flow - er seeds, drink - in' lots of car - rot juice and soak - in' up rays. But at

night I'd have these won - der - ful dreams: some kind of sen - su - ous

DOES YOUR CHEWING GUM LOSE ITS FLAVOR ON THE BEDPOST OVERNIGHT?

Words and Music by Billy Rose,
Marty Bloom and Ernest Breuer
Arranged by Dan Coates

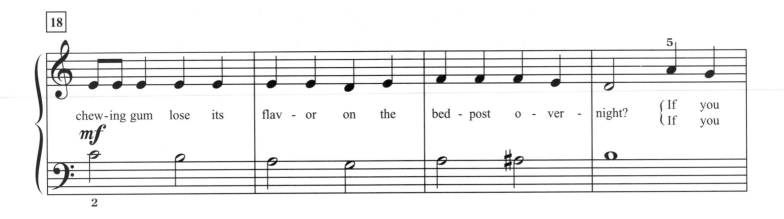

18

chew-ing gum lose its flav - or on the bed-post o - ver - night? {If you / If you

22

chew it in the morn - ing, will it be too hard to bite? Can't you

pull it out like rub - ber will it snap right back and bite? If you

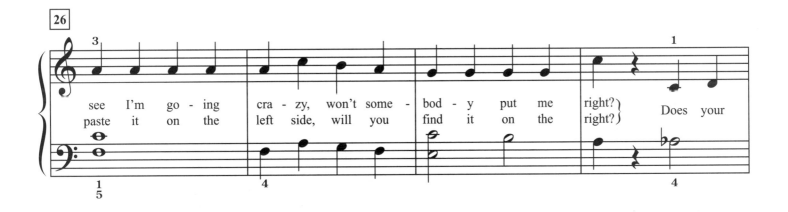

26

see I'm go - ing cra - zy, won't some - bod - y put me right?}

paste it on the left side, will you find it on the right?} Does your

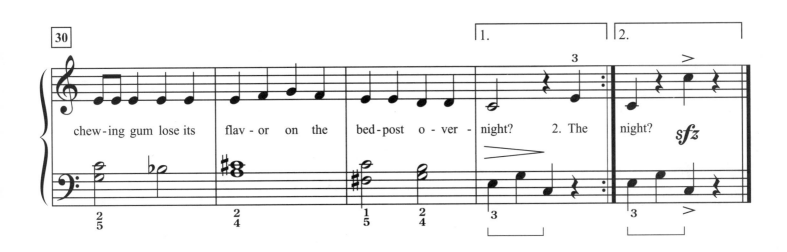

30

chew-ing gum lose its flav - or on the bed-post o - ver - night? 2. The night?

DOODLE DOO DOO

Words and Music by
Art Kassel and Mel Stitzel
Arranged by Dan Coates

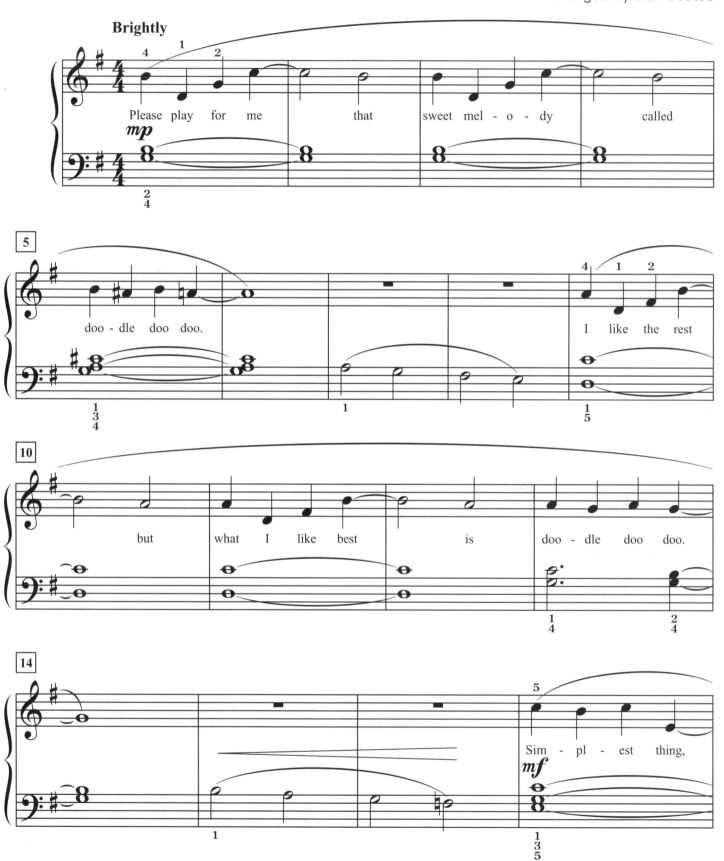

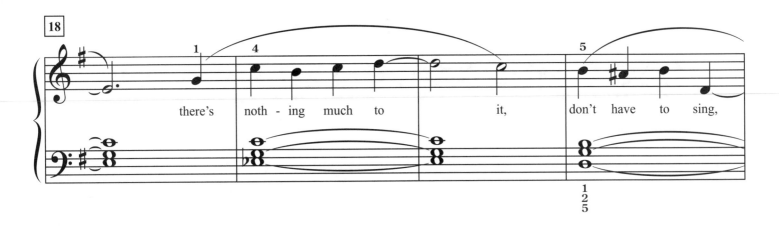

there's noth - ing much to it, don't have to sing,

just doo - dle doo doo it. I love it so

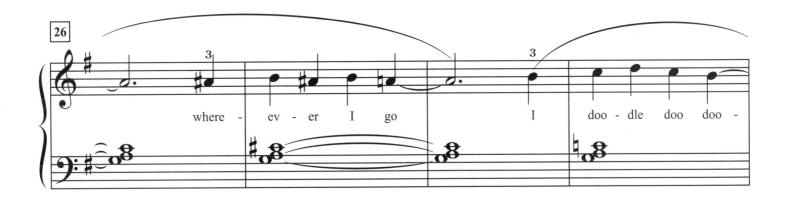

where - ev - er I go I doo - dle doo doo -

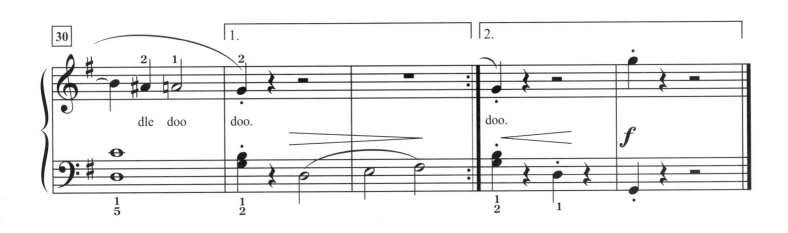

dle doo doo. doo.

HELLO MUDDAH, HELLO FADDUH!

Music by Lou Busch
Words by Allan Sherman
Arranged by Dan Coates

Moderately, in two

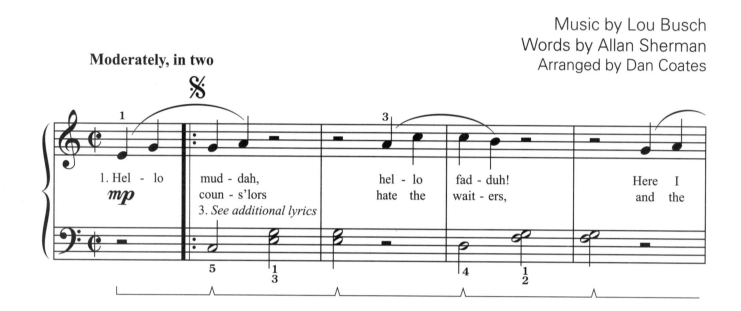

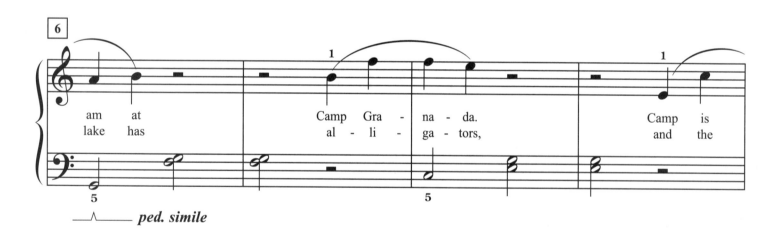

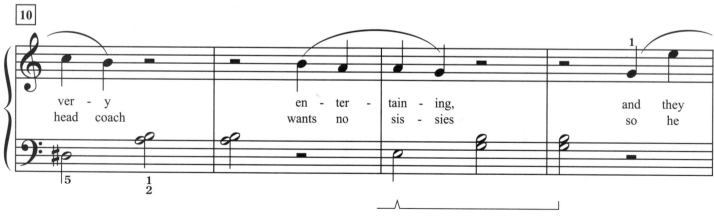

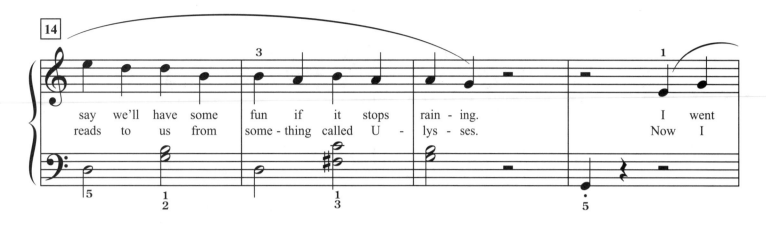

say we'll have some / fun if it stops / rain - ing. / I went
reads to us from / some - thing called U - / lys - ses.

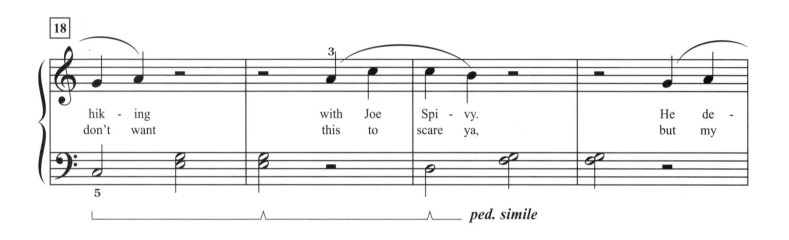

hik - ing / with Joe / Spi - vy. / He de -
don't want / this to / scare ya, / but my

ped. simile

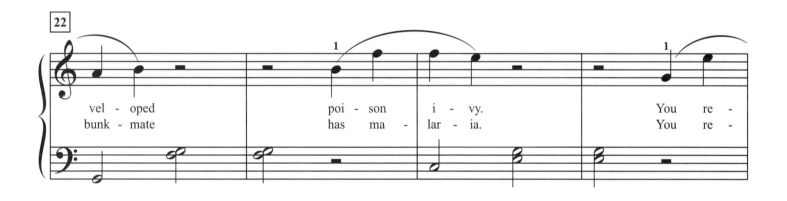

vel - oped / poi - son i - vy. / You re -
bunk - mate / has ma - lar - ia. / You re -

to Coda ⊕

mem - ber / Leo - nard Skin - ner? / He got
mem - ber / Jeff - rey Hard - y? / They're a -

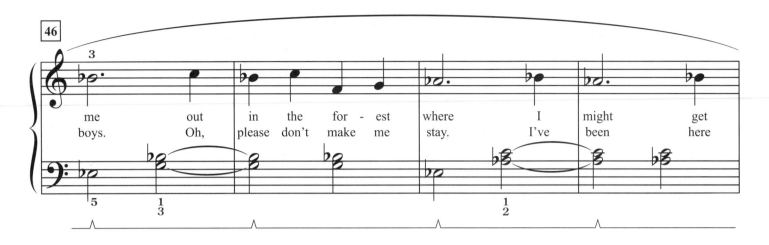

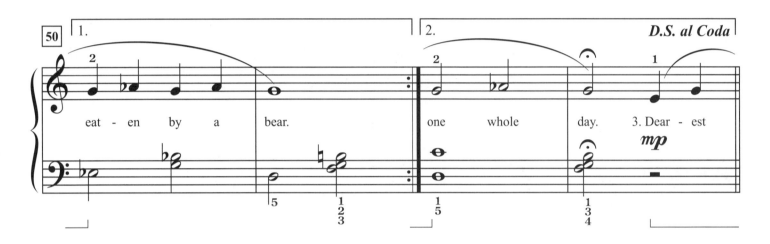

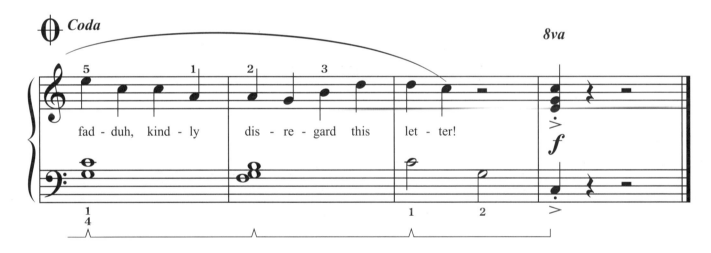

Verse 3:
Dearest fadduh, darling muddah,
How's my precious little bruddah?
Let me come home if you miss me.
I would even let Aunt Bertha hug and kiss me.
Wait a minute, it stopped hailing.
Guys are swimming, guys are sailing!
Playing baseball, gee, that's better.
Muddah, fadduh, kindly disregard this letter!

ITSY BITSY TEENIE WEENIE YELLOW POLKA DOT BIKINI

Words and Music by
Paul J. Vance and Lee Pockriss
Arranged by Dan Coates

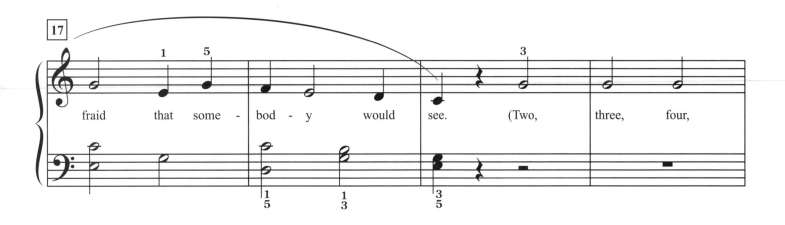

fraid that some - bod - y would see. (Two, three, four,

tell the peo - ple what she wore.) It was an

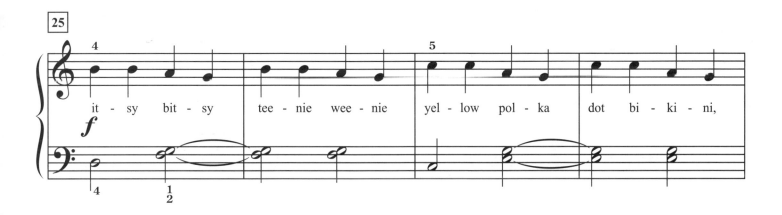

it - sy bit - sy tee - nie wee - nie yel - low pol - ka dot bi - ki - ni,

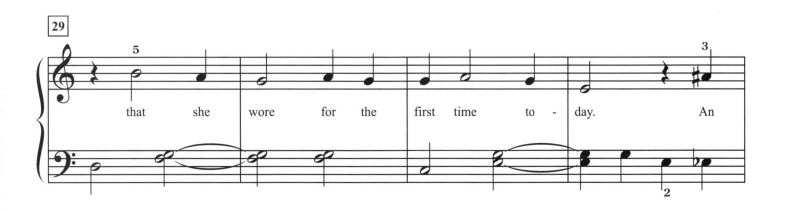

that she wore for the first time to - day. An

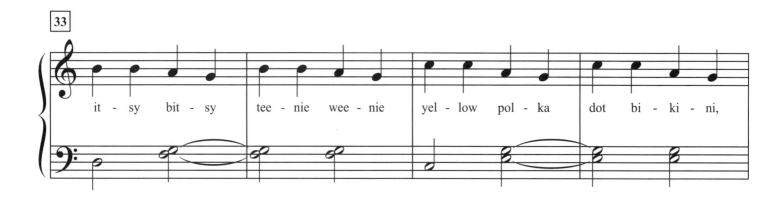

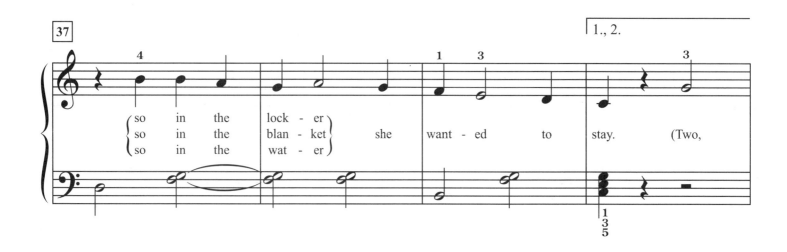

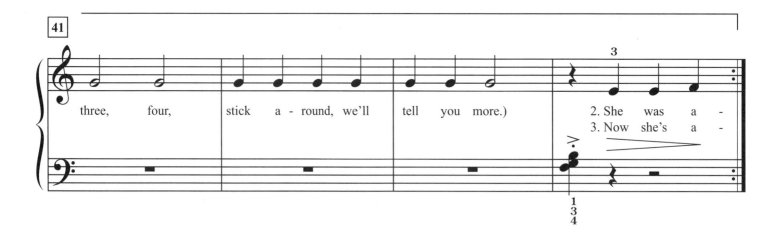

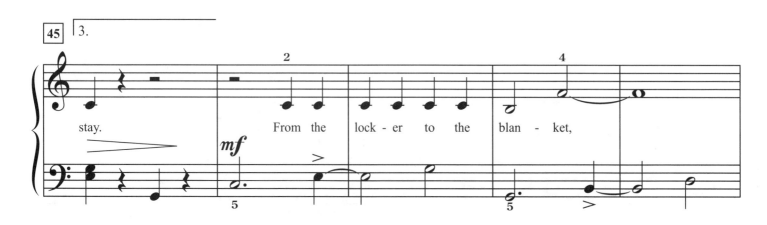

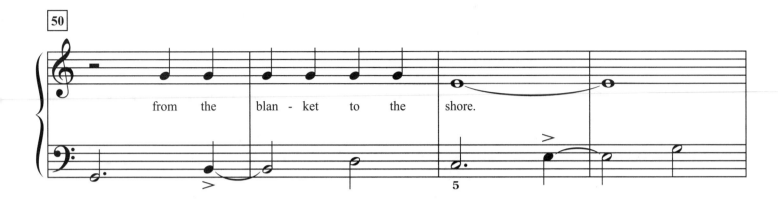

from the blan - ket to the shore.

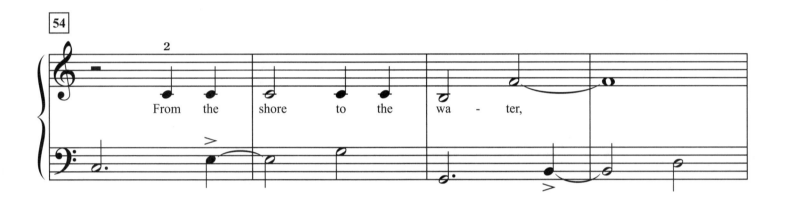

From the shore to the wa - ter,

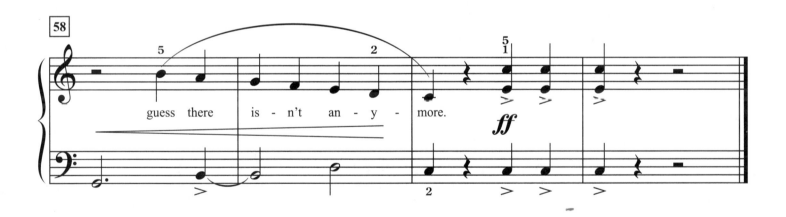

guess there is - n't an - y - more.

ff

Verse 2:
She was afraid to come out in the open,
And so a blanket around her she wore.
She was afraid to come out in the open,
And so she sat bundled up on the shore.
(Two, three, four, tell the people what she wore.)

Verse 3:
Now she's afraid to come out of the water,
And I wonder what she's gonna do.
Now she's afraid to come out of the water,
And the poor little girl's turning blue.
(Two, three, four, tell the people what she wore.)

JEEPERS CREEPERS

Words by Johnny Mercer
Music by Harry Warren
Arranged by Dan Coates

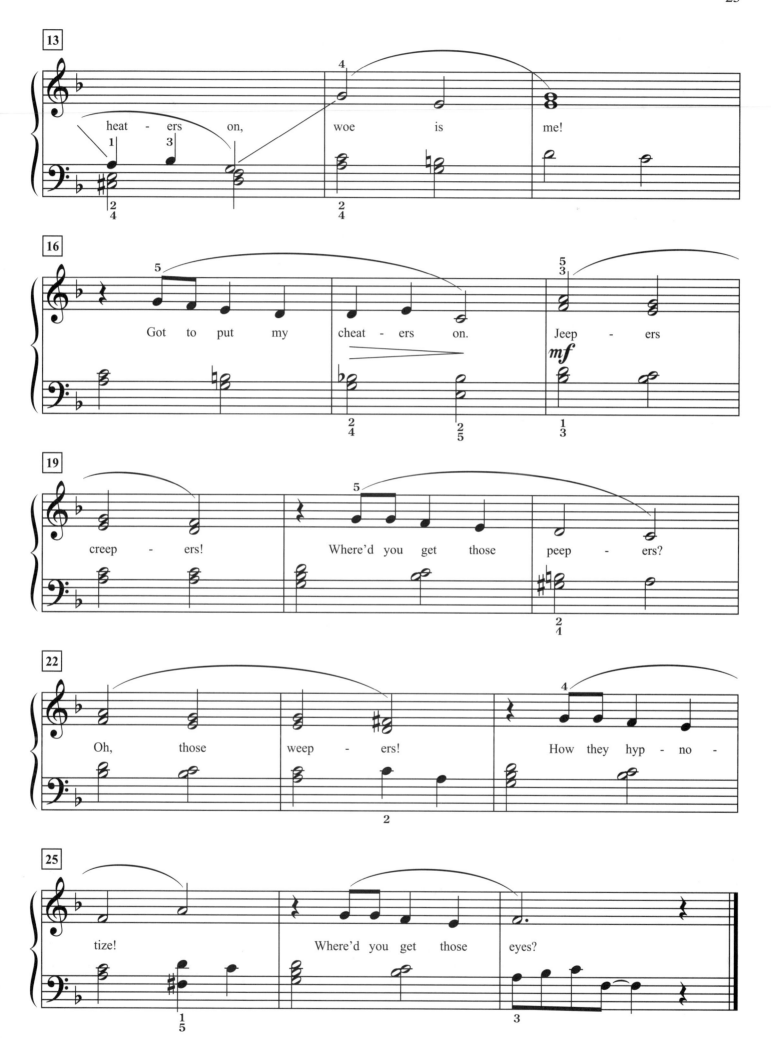

LITTLE SIR ECHO

Original Version by
Laura R. Smith and J.S. Fearis
Words and Revised Arrangement by
Adele Girard and Joe Marsala
Arranged by Dan Coates

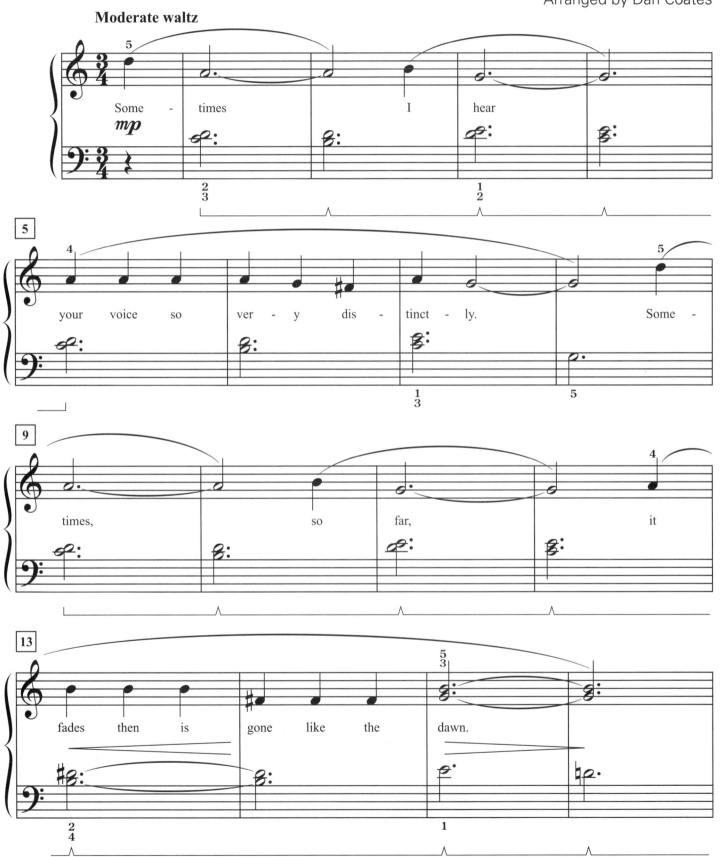

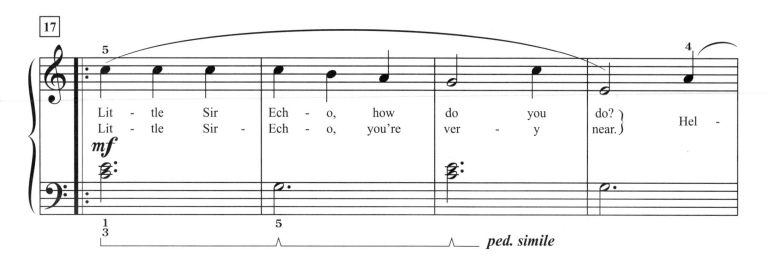

Lit - tle Sir - Ech - o, how do you do? }
Lit - tle Sir - Ech - o, you're ver - y near. } Hel -

mf

ped. simile

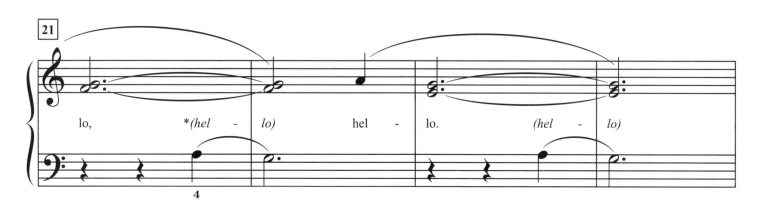

lo, *(hel - lo)* hel - lo. *(hel - lo)*

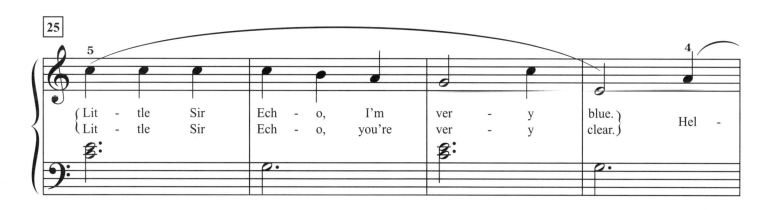

{ Lit - tle Sir Ech - o, I'm ver - y blue. }
{ Lit - tle Sir Ech - o, you're ver - y clear. } Hel -

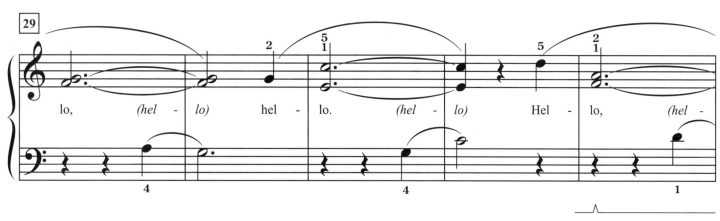

lo, *(hel - lo)* hel - lo. *(hel - lo)* Hel - lo, *(hel -*

* echo

34 _lo)_ hel - lo. _(hel - lo)_ Won't you come

38 o - ver and play? _(and play)_ You're a nice lit - tle

mf

42 fel - low, I know by your voice, but you're al - ways so

46 far a - way. _(a - way)_ way. _(a - way)_

mp rit.

WHEN BANANA SKINS ARE FALLING (I'LL COME SLIDING BACK TO YOU)

Words and Music by Al Frazzini,
Paul Defrank and Irving Mills
Arranged by Dan Coates

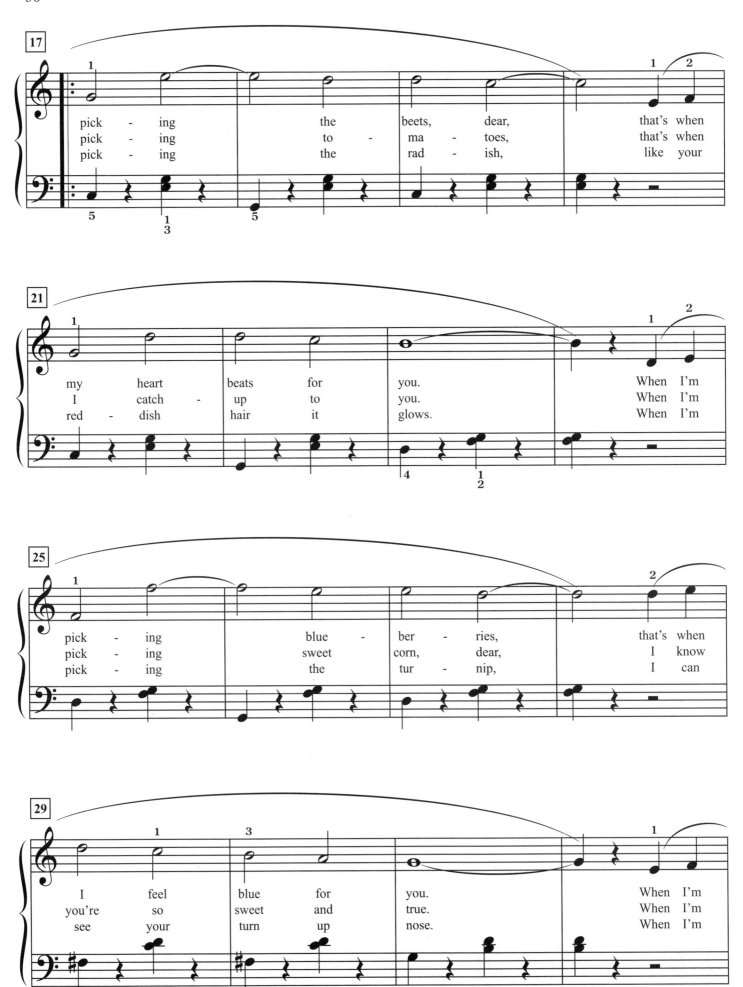

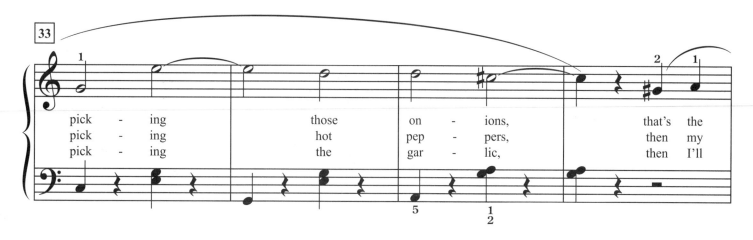

pick - ing those on - ions, that's the
pick - ing hot pep - pers, then my
pick - ing the gar - lic, then I'll

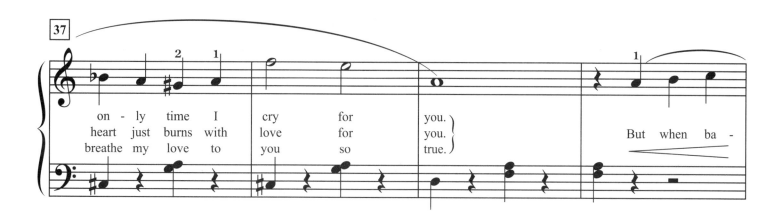

on - ly time I cry for you.
heart just burns with love for you.
breathe my love to you so true.

But when ba -

na - na skins are fall - ing, I'll come slid - ing

back to you.

1., 2.
you.
you.

2. When I'm
3. When I'm

3.
you.